sticks 70

poems of life & love

DALLAS GATLIN

TATE PUBLISHING *& Enterprises*

"Seventy Sticks" by Dallas Gatlin

Copyright © 2006 by Dallas Gatlin. All rights reserved.

Published in the United States of America
by Tate Publishing, LLC
127 East Trade Center Terrace
Mustang, OK 73064
(888) 361-9473

Book design copyright © 2006 by Tate Publishing, LLC. All rights reserved.

No part of this publication may be reproduced, stored in a retrieval system or transmitted in any way by any means, electronic, mechanical, photocopy, recording or otherwise without the prior permission of the author except as provided by USA copyright law.

ISBN: 1-5988644-8-3

060616

endorsements:

Seventy Sticks will help you recall the way you felt during those special moments of your life. It is written from a faithful heart with a cleverness and breadth of knowledge that every reader will appreciate and enjoy. It will leave you with an understanding of a full and meaningful life that is built upon a love for God and family."

BRIAN M. MITCHELL, PH. D
Senior Research Scientist, OptiMetrics
Ann Arbor, Michigan

Pick up *Seventy Sticks* and enjoy an incredible narrative journey, as Dallas Gatlin, creatively guides you toward a fuller experience of all that life can offer you. Dallas is my friend, a gifted teacher and word-smith; I encourage you to immerse yourself in LIFE through this poet's hearty embracing of love, faith and doubt. I have learned from watching and listening to Dallas; now I can learn by reading his poems.

DR. MIKE KITSKO
Spiritual Formation Pastor
Central Church of the Nazarene
Flint, Michigan

Seventy Sticks is a compelling look at life that will have you rereading many of the verses. Even the well-read may need a dictionary to interpret some of the words, and a second reading often reveals more understanding and insight. What stands out is the author's passion for life... a life that is focused on God, wife and family. As he shares his thoughts and insights, Mr. Gatlin forces us to take a look at our own lives. "Why am I here? How do I love and What do I believe?" are common thoughts as you read the verse. "There's life in the art of the finish" is a fitting conclusion to an enjoyable and insightful book of poetry.

MIKE TAUBITZ
OHS-Manager
General Motors Corporation
March 26, 2006

The thoughtful reader will find *70 Sticks* a delightful indulgence to satisfy the soul. Dallas Gatlin brings to his audience insight and a breath of fresh air on the poetry scene. From the depths of his faith the author entertains with short and crisp items like *Perfidious* and entrances the reader's deepest yearnings with the soul searching clarity of *Walking Due East*. *70 Sticks* is a collection you won't want to miss!

DONALD N. REED, JR.
Professor, Michigan State University

If you want to feel a kindred spirit, to laugh out loud, to think deeply pick up *70 Sticks*. In the poems of Dallas Gatlin, you'll discover a writer whose passion and honesty strike home to the heart....

Thomas Loyola, DMin
Senior Pastor, Evangelical Free Church of Clinton

Poetry should be savored; flavors experienced one small piece at a time. From the first page to the last, the poems in 70 Sticks became a collection of appetizers that required me to treat the book as a full course meal. And contrary to feeling stuffed at the end of the sitting, I only wanted more. Dallas Gatlin has produced one very gratifying meal that will satisfy the hunger in all of us of for those eternal needs of love, hope and promise.

Jeff Pratt, PhD
Superintendent, Swartz Creek Community Schools
April 10, 2006

dedication

To Nola, my love and my life, without whose spark there would be no fire; and to the other four flames who burn in my heart: Nate, Nic, Em, and Ty.

acknowledgment

Dr. John Spencer, who resides now in heaven, but who taught many at Kalamazoo College how to seek God by asking the tough questions; Mrs. Dorothy Stahly, my English teacher, who with positive and patient determination inspired me and countless others to write; Mr. Robert Pettengill and Ms. Nancy Peters, who graciously reviewed my manuscript; the great staff at Tate Publishing for their guidance and professionalism; and Darwin and Betty Gatlin, whose love led to an ushering of eight souls into this world—the sixth one being me.

Contents

- ESTHESIA 19
- THE KISS 20
- CLOSE TO THE DANGEROUS CLIFFS 21
- A TOWN CALLED USUFRUCT 22
- UNDER THE WILLOW 23
- THE FEET OF JUDAS 24
- PERFIDIOUS 27
- THE IDIOT GARDENER 28
- SUNFLOWER SOLDIERS 29
- OUR QUILT 30
- GILLESPIE'S PATH 31
- TOTAL ABSOLUTION 32
- MY LITTLE GIRL 33
- TELL ME WHO YOU ARE 34
- LIANA 35
- MAN, BIKE, AND RADIO 36
- WALKING DUE EAST 38
- SEE IT 39
- YOU ARE MY WIGAN 40
- THE ROQUE TREE 41
- A HOPEFUL HEART 42
- PULLING UP STAKES 43
- HEARTS FOREVER 44
- MACULA LUTEA 45
- JUST IN TIME 46
- LOOSE THE FETTERED DREAMS 47
- A TREASURE TROVE 48
- BE NOT BEDRAGGLED 49
- COFFEE WITH NOLA 51
- BOANERGES CUP 52

FUTURES BRIGHT AND BOLD	53
DINOSAUR TRACKS	54
ON THAT DAY	55
HONESTLY	57
MY PEARLS	58
THE CANDLE'S BURNING	60
SHIVERING	61
ONE SHORT LIFE	62
RESCUE DAMNED	63
JUST FOOLING	64
RAPTURE DAY	65
WHEN ADAM SINNED	66
BROOD OF VIPERS	68
WITH YOUR MAKER DANCE	70
THE MISSIVE	71
I AM LOST	72
YOU FILL MY HOLLOW	73
THE CHASE	74
TWELVE MEN	75
PLANKS	76
LIGHT YEARS FROM EARTH	77
AN UN-GELDED SAILOR	78
HAND IN GLOVE	79
YOUNG LOVE	82
GREEN EYES LOVELY	84
HOW ABOUT ME AND THEN YOU	85
DJELLABA	86
A COMITIA OF TWO	87
THE POET DIED	88
THE POET LIVES	89
THE RESURRECTION	90
LAST PLACE IN A FAST RACE	91
WHY THE WHINING?	92
I LOVE THE RAIN	94
LIKE WINDMILLS	95
HEARTLESS MOUNTAIN	96
ALON	97

Enough	98
First Kisses	99
John's Pass	100
Joy of My Life	101
Living Lightly	102
A Persistent Suitor	103
The Skeptic's Sip	104
Curled Under All Around	106
Not Enough Rhyme	107
Death, I Smile	108
A Violet Hue	109
Homemade Chains	110
Chancy the Cat	111
A Phrase Rings	112
A Martingale	114
A Plaited Omnipotent Love	115
Can it Be?	116
Dance in the House by the Hill	117
My Teacher's Words	118
Your Face a Song	119
Fly with You	120
In Our Garden	121
Sapphire Star	122
Wonder What the Fairness Is?	124
While the Cicadas Sleep	125
The Stranger's Lair	126
The Voice	127
The Solitary Vase	128
Saints' Hopeful Gaze	129
Rainbow's Breeze	130
Then and Now	131
My Flower	132
Nathanael	133
Nickel-dime	134
The Emily Rose	136
Ty	137
Settle in Home	138

Two Worlds Spinning	139
Sharing Sheron	140
The Christmas Bacchant	141
A Tennessee Farm	142
Sand Pebble Sabbath	143
The Scenarist	145
Nola My Passion	146
Never a Day	147
An Innocent Rebirth	148
Poison Leaves	149
Violet Flowers	150
The Other Side	151
Nolita Oregano	152
Your Turn to Speak	153
To Be Me	154
On My Chiffonier	155
The Whistling Wind	156
The Death Wish Squirrel	157
A Spectator's Cage	158
Walking with You	159
You Wear My Ring	160
A Zoo for You	161
Libeccio	162
Leave it to Me	163
$E = mc^2$	164
Saturday Morning	165
The Daily Push	166
An Island?	167
Reality Check	169
A Life Well Lived	170
A Number Between	171
Caught Between Two Seeds	172
My Firefly	173
The Day Has Come	174
Now Is Coming	175
Free from Niggling	176
Dirge of Dogs	177

SIMPLE THINGS	178
SPEAKING FRANKLY	179
THE WINGS THAT I GREW	181
70 STICKS	182
CELESTE CLOTURE	183
DEATH IN A SESAME SEED BUN	184
IN SOME WAYS	185
CAMOUFLAGED COOKIES	186
INSIDE GOD	187
LEAVE GOLD BEHIND	188
NADI	189
PEOPLE ARE	190
PROMISES UNKEMPT	191
PURPLE TARGET	192
SHE PROVIDES	193
THE COSMOS QUESTION	194
WHAT DO I KNOW?	195
WHO CREATED WHOM?	196
THE ART OF THE FINISH	198

introduction

"The length of our days is seventy years—or eighty if we have the strength" (Psalm 90:10 NIV). We're born, we live, we die; this book is about the "live" part. These poems describe romances and victories, breakups and defeats, celebrations of life, and the fear of death. Most of all, the overriding theme is one of hope; a hope grounded both in the seen and the unseen, the known and the vaguely known. I hope that in these verses you see some of yourself, your losses, and your triumphs. My earnest desire is that you will find life and hope in the one who has placed us here for awhile to live and to struggle, to hurt and to hope, and eventually to fall to the ground and die like a seed that will spring forth to new life.

Esthesia

Esthesia
What an odd choice of names
For one who so easily broke my heart
It's not easy to go numbly through life
Cutting through friendships with a dull butcher's knife
How am I supposed to make a fresh start?
Esthesia, an odd choice of names

Esthesia
Who brought you to me?
For tearing and shredding the cords of my breast
It's not easy to recover from the burn of your nails
Inflicted through armor that fits but then fails
How am I supposed to wear this thin vest?
Esthesia, who brought you to me?

Esthesia
What an odd choice of names
You who arrived with your emotions all out
It's not easy to adjust so quickly to your true exposed self
Taking you seriously then watching you morph to a mutated elf
How am I supposed to love and then lout?
Esthesia, what and odd choice of names

The Kiss

A look, a smile, a wink
Hearts seeking
Connection, fantasy raging
Desire waiting

A call, a question, acceptance
Hearts racing
Love waiting, anticipation
Dreams overtaking

The day, the hour, the moment
Paradise Beach
Slow walking, hands clasping
A fall to the grass

Fears rising, desire winning
Hearts pounding
A look; a smile; surrender
The Kiss

Close To The Dangerous Cliffs

Far from the reaches of sinister doubt
Yet close to the dangerous cliffs
Far from the lion who walks about
Far from the spiritual rifts

Far from the altars where ministers pout
Far from the winnowing sifts
Far from the teacher who yells and shouts
Far from the ritual gifts

Far from the creature I daily tout
Far from the ill informed "ifs"
Far from the mask, now inside out
Yet close to the dangerous cliffs

A Town Called Usufruct

I live today in Usufruct
A town not far from you
Amazing graceful streets unwind
To the "Square of Redbrick Hue"

I love to walk in Usufruct
The sounds are sweet to hear
A wretched man strolls in the square
So lost but somehow near

I found a man in Usufruct
A wretched blind man he
His sight returned in Usufruct
The blind man's name was me

Under The Willow

Under the willow a vast world is hidden
Under its branches strange creatures conspire
Under the willow, God reached out to meet me
And told me some secrets that lit a great fire

Under the willow, my mother came to me
Under its twig-house she taught me to sing
Under the willow, I sang my first chorus
And nature danced with us, to the rhythm of the swing

Under the willow, the rain could not reach me
Under its canopy, all creatures were safe
Under the willow, I dreamed my first vision
To set off and wander, a vagabond waif

Under the willow, I met my first lady
Under its spell, I kissed my first maid
Under the willow, she came closer to me
And I sang her that chorus, as my lady laid

The Feet Of Judas

Quietly he rose
Carefully, as though
Something hard weighed on his mind
Toward Peter he bowed low

Stripping nearly naked
Towel tied 'round his waist
First him, and then another when
His eyes turned toward my face

Perhaps I should have risen up
No host to serve or wait
Perhaps I should have thought of it
But then is was too late

So I let him loose my sandals
He dropped them near the bag
And raised my feet up to his lap
And caressed them with a rag

My eyes fixed on his stare right then
A kind stare knowing truth
It nearly took my breath away I
Succumbed to him like Ruth

But his hands were kind, and so his look
He washed and dried me there
He set my feet upon the floor
I felt so naked, bare

And suddenly he disappeared
My tears made him but a blur
And as he came back into view
His motions measured, sure

His outstretched arms crossed over
To John and then to James
With simple abba tenderness
Not like a judge who blames

He said some words, we dipped some bread
His hand nudged against my thumb
I almost changed my mind right then
And then my sense went numb

"Go quickly" came the words to me
They cut me like a knife
I rose and stumbled to the street
The last road of my life

I wonder what that all just meant
Though part I think I knew
But on I ran with feet once clean
Through dusty streets I flew

I ran and told the priests to come
And brought them to the place
And all my friends there with him stared
Right through my dusty face

I kissed him then, and pulled away
From words that stung like fire
And ran from there with dirty feet
My ankles tied in "wire"

I ran until I could not breathe
My feet then stopped to see
A darkened sky, a hilly place
A ready, solid tree

I'll jump from there, and then I'll hang
Negating my senseless birth
My life ebbs out from under me
My feet touch not the earth.

Perfidious

Perfidious
Thou art insidious
Lurking as you do in your hair

Perfidious
Someone hideous
Tricking me to think that you care

Perfidious and
Almost fastidious
Condemning me for all my laissez-faire

Perfidious yes
Your nature invidious
Like a child-phobic contented au pair

Perfidious
May I call you Perfidious?
A fitting name for one so unfair

The Idiot Gardener

I plant the seeds and enjoy it so
That I can never seem to stop, you know?
I plant in your plot and in mine
Whoever's plot is always fine
I think of it and dream the same
Of seeds all planted in my name
But once they sprout, I've had enough
For gardening is all too tough
I'd have to stop the other things
I do in life, the joy it brings
And so for now I'll just plant seeds
And pull up the plants, when they have needs

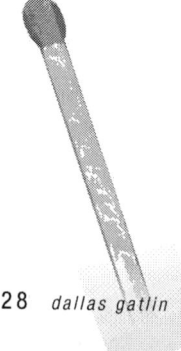

Sunflower Soldiers

Sunflower soldiers march in formation,
To the beat of a heavenly call
Freedom fighters from a friendly nation,
Guarding the summer from fall

Now green leaves spread upward in sweet jubilation,
To the charismatic Maker palms raise
The wind chimes in with sweet supplications,
And heaven lets loose its rivers of praise

Soon black faces smile in rapture-elation,
For the hum of the pollen-packed drone
Each one flying from station to station,
Feet softly landing to deliver life home

Petals shine outward, in controlled conflagration,
Returning their light to the Source
Sharing a life-giving burning sensation,
A marriage in Heaven, to Death a divorce

Our Quilt

The house was small when it was built
So cute and full of life
The quilt was laid on Grandma's chair
Where lovely sat my wife

We talked and walked about that house
And cared for it with joy
The days passed by invisibly
And then we had our boy

Our son was blue when he was born
But soon was full of life
With quilt he rocked in Grandma's chair
Where lovely sang my wife

Our second son and then our girl
Born in a larger place
Both snuggled close in that old quilt
Each with a lovely face

And then one day came youngest son
To yet a larger home
We wrapped him up in that fine quilt
The final patchwork sown

A house now large is home to us
My Bride and me alone
And we sit cuddled in that quilt
The patchwork of our home

Gillespie's Path

Daylong swims on the bank of the creek
Leeches delight at the taste of my feet
A good sort of "drained" feeling
Sits on my chest
But the sun's going down
So there's no time to rest

Across the wood bridge, I sprint for the path
And stop to watch ghost cows enjoying their bath
A strange sort of haunting
But not one to fear
Grabs hold of my spirit
And speaks in my ear

Warm friendly words in synch with the breeze
Ride 'long Gillespie's path with truth-telling ease
A safe sort of calmness
Revisits this place
Each time when I come here
And ask Him to race

Total Absolution

Cut the sky, knife of reason to the bone
Sacrifice the superstitious calf
Bleed the neck at the ready altar stone
Killed on my behalf

Drain dogma from the well-fed creature lain
Flow ruby red lifeless blood
Spill this comfort down the drain
Burn the carcass with over-flooded wood

Wait my sin-sick heart for healthy rhythm
Quivering now with uncertain end
Synchronize the truth as given
Beat with life and joy again

Pierce my soul keen knife of purpose seen
Slay the lifeless demon mind
Bleed my self-locked fleshy prison clean
Leave a well-lit room behind

Pour cold doubts from brand new veins of hope
Flow blue haunting fixed solution
Faith and Truth remove the aged, man-made Pope
Granting total absolution.

My Little Girl

Sleep my lady, sleep for a while
Sleep with your tender, little girl smile
Sleep while the world turns it back to the sun
Sleep with summer sweet dreams
And with little girls run

Run in the sunshine so warm on your face
Run to the little boy in the tree by that place
Run with your hands up, hair all blowing back
Run from the little girls,
But say you'll be back

Climb to the little boy so high on that limb
Climb up to kiss him 'fore the light gets too dim
Climb up with black shoes hugging each step
Climb up and tell him
Where your secrets are kept

Wake to the morning all fresh with delight
Wake from your sweet dreams that you had last night
Wake to your little boy who's near you in bed
Wake up my little girl
Your little boy said!

Tell Me Who You Are

Express yourself
Tell me who you are
Hide nothing but the pieces
That tell all you're a star

Take a chance
Speak of all the things
Things you've always hidden
Deep within your dreams

Attack
Kill the thoughts you fear
Fears that need not live
To taunt your sharpened spear

Live on
Strut your inner gold
Walk with all your pages open
A romance to be told

Forget it
That story you have saved
Let the old news die today
That's had you so enslaved

Breathe
Take your new life in
Smell the deep and sweet release
Of starting new again

LIANA

Liana clings to growing giants
Rooted deep in oceans green
Clings so hopeful for protection
A holding up, a holding up

Liana roots her own life anchor
Deep into the earthen mattes
Digging for a life to serve her
A holding up

Liana sings in pictures' wisdom
Deep whole notes and higher eighths
Singing in a silent solo
A holding up, a holding up

Liana soothes herself with fingers
Fingers reaching to the vines
Fingers holding to a treasure
A holding up

Man, Bike, and Radio

A radio rests by his side
As he sits there on the bench
A Gulf side path
His carpet makes
His air
A fishy stench

His bike leans next the post nearby
That lights this bench at night
His bench, his bike he
Makes his way
His radio his light

His basket full of bottles brings
Fresh batteries to power
His radio
So he can pass
From hour to dreadful hour

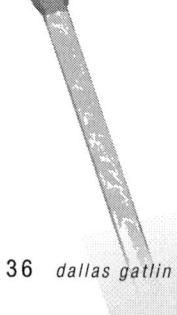

No strangers stop to talk to him
As he sits or rides or stares
Into each face
He peers perchance
To sense if someone cares

A voice speaks for a moment now
As the hour passes three
It blankets him
A daily friend
Not one like you or me

The news is not all bad today
On WXNO
It speaks to him
From this bench again
Man, bike, and radio

Walking Due East

Walking due east
With the sun on my face
Is just the intention
I think should replace
All the cautious wandering
That looks so good on paper
But is just the sort of plan
That turns substance to vapor

Flying straight up
With the sun in my eyes
Is just the invention
I want to resize
My small little plan
That looks so good in theory
But is just the sort of musing
That makes the hopeful weary

Dreaming wide open
With the sun on my brain
Is just the extension
I need to regain
That childlike dependence
That looks so good to many
But is just the sort of innocence
That lives in hardly any

See It

See it
Hold the vision there
There where your heart beats
Hold it, in the palm of your life
Watch it
See the fission where
Where your dreams live
Snatch it
Catch the decision lair
Lair of surrender
Let it
Let the Thing hold you
You who it knows well
Take it
Take the revision made
Made of your heart
Feel it
Feel the deep scission there
There where your soul rests
Embrace it
Let it complete you
Complete with deep love
Love for your Maker
Take it

You Are My Wigan

You are my wigan
I have known this for some time now
I have understood it from before I knew it out loud
In my head
You ring my limp weakness like a sheepdog
Circles its flock; you brace my life against
The surprise winds like a stake by a thin tree
You are strength, but not starch
I know not what I would do without you
Except to be less than half of what we are together
You are my wigan, my vertebraic consistency
Giving straight form to what otherwise would be
An amoebic, protoplasmic, digester of whatever
Happened by; you are my wigan, my helper
My wife

dallas gatlin

The Roque Tree

It dared me to do it, to climb
So skinny it was, so high
A stick of a tree
But formidable
A foe and friend, and a poke

It called me to scale it, to reach
So tall in the wind, it whipped
Like a menacing snake
But beautiful
An angelical demon, a style baroque

It begged me to finish, to fly
So ready to summit, to reign
On top of the world
But humble
A cover for fear, like a cloak

It held me up there, to see
So skinny and strong, so high
A stick of a tree
But formidable
A foe and a friend, to provoke

It urged me this day, to play
So tall in the wind, it whipped
It a mallet of fear
I return
A ball in the game, like roque

A Hopeful Heart

Fastened closely to the open wounded heel
Is a shameful mark of separation
A reminder of a warning not heeded
Of a word of wisdom, thought to be unneeded
Of a loneliness now drowning a previously hopeful heart

Measured wearily is the paradise lost
A place of safe contentment now but a disappearing misty thought
A reminder of a rogue anchor voluntarily cut loose
Smashing about on a chanceless bow as waves of torment crash
Immersing smooth seas in an ever widening, thrashing pool of despair

Gnashing teeth hold tightly to the only thing you can
While some brave soul dispenses measures long ago determined
A reminder of an impotent soul, proudly boasting
'Bout a word of wisdom, thought to be unneeded
And a hero captain, immersing courageously to grab 'hold the anchor lost

Fastened closely to wounded hands extended
A bridge to paradise made of lively palms
A reminder of a peaceful love unheeded
Of a word of wisdom that called and pleaded
Of a wounded heel that crushed a serpent's head, and restored a hopeful heart

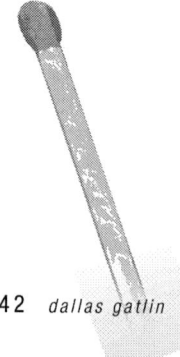

Pulling Up Stakes

Crooked row
Where was the planning?
Once again, by the seat of the pants
Too quick to go
The daylight was fleeting
The first step is *always* to water the plants

Maybe next time
There'll be more thinking
A little more thought, before planting the seeds
Too quick to act
Perhaps it was cheating
I thought I could start, by pulling the weeds

Lucky for me
The day is now ending
Once again, erasing mistakes
Too quick to sleep
My dreams are repeating
The starting to build, by pulling up stakes

Hearts Forever

Hearts together
Hearts ablaze
Hearts now merging
Hearts in phase
Hearts connecting
Hearts amazed
Hearts now swelling
Hearts' vision dazed
Hearts forever
Hearts entwine
Hearts in love
Both yours and mine

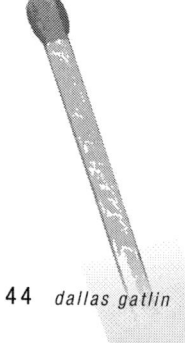

Macula Lutea

Macula Lutea
That's where I want to live
In back where you can see a
Single focus and forgive
Forgive the many sins against
Yourself, against your friends
Forgive yourself for things for which
God's love has made amends
Forgive yourself for lying
Forgive yourself for lust
Forgive yourself for misdirecting
Life respecting trust
Forgive your friend for hurting you
Forgive him and move on
Cast the cut so far away
Your thoughts can't land upon
The salty wound that calls you
To recall the moment when
The slice cut to the bone right through
And you lashed back at your friend
Consider that your author has
Suffered wounds pierced by *your* sins
Remember that he took it when
You had no able friends
Remember when you look on him
To see your life renewed
A pinpoint focus on your source
Your enemies subdued
Macula lutea
The spot to see the best
A place where you can see a
Single focus and find rest

Just in Time

Just in time to breathe some air
Where I am I know not where
Light so bright it hurts my eyes
What is light?
My new voice cries

Something warm is holding me
Warm not wet like used to be
Tight so tight enfolding me
What is tight?
Just wait and see

Just in time to hear a voice
Almost tried to make a choice
Choice so hard it hurt my heart
What is choice?
A place to start

Something new appears to me
I'm not you, and you're not me
Something strong inside my head
What is strong?
To choose instead

Just in time to choose instead
To breathe and live is life I read
A life so sweet it's holds to me
What is sweet?
My choice you see?

Loose the Fettered Dreams

Loose the fettered dreams of fading youth
Cleanse the wrinkles from long worried brows
Shave the army of attriting hairs
With stoic, chiseled face march out with brave new risky vows

Laugh at weakened knees and aching joints
Run with reckless joy toward rising suns
Drink from founts of optimistic schemes
With deafened ears ignore the safe and measured paths of cloistered nuns

Smother now the voice that always calls you back
Tell it loud to finally take its place in Hell's abyss
Watch for God to show His lovely, warrior face
And sing with armor dropped and arms stretched out to hold His mighty fist

Let the battle stop when He appears
Bow with healed knees and youthful limbs
Shine with all the stars that now have found their place
And with the light now given illuminate the path with silent Hymns

A Treasure Trove

A treasure trove in treatise write
All locked away in thoughts by night
Secure them with poetic key
From people reading for précis

Sweep them under rug to show
A cleaner stepping place to go
Knowing someday some will find
A playful reading for the mind

Taking time to sit and think
To dream in colors blue and pink
Noting clouds before the rain
Seeing with red shepherd's cane

Treasure trove in words refine
And sing them softly line-by-line
Hum the words to tunes you know
And set the silver cord aglow

And when the cord begins to tear
To treasure trove of words repair
A pillowed place to lay your head
A place of pink, and blue, and red

BE NOT BEDRAGGLED

Thou who art the draggled one
Come out from the mud
Bedraggled by thy master
Who cares not thou art a son

A son of highest calling
A son of noble breed
A commoner of course thou art
But yet of perfect seed

Come whilst thou still
Are caked in mud
Take root in circumstance
And from thy place
Where thou art now
Take hold thy second chance

Thy real Master loves thee
And grants thee this escape
So stand thou up and take it now
Accept His hand of grace

Thou who art the draggled one
Your master loves thee not
He only wants to watch thee writhe
In this thy cursed lot

So bid him his deserved leave
And stand now to thy feet
And cleanse thyself in showers clean
From heaven full and deep

And when thou hast enjoyed thy bath
Let joy flood through thy flesh
And cheer the sunrise of your soul
All clean, and good, and fresh

Thy Master new, He loves thee
Bedraggled though you were
He cares to see thee walking tall
He loves thee to be sure

Coffee with Nola

Sunny fall, have it all
Sipping coffee in the mall
Sharing words crocheted with ribbons
Adding color to white-lie fibbin's

Funny tales, the stories' whale
Sharing thoughts of yellowed mail
Loving life's parlayed little fancies
Loving Nolas, Anns, and Nancys

Wonder women, all are mine
Sipping mochas, feelin' fine
Wasting time with reckless ease
Pass the coffee, sweetie, please?

Boanerges Cup

Boanerges, Boanerges
Sons of Thunder two
Salome your mother
Must wonder what He'll do
Will He make you powerful?
Share honor with His name
Or will you be forgotten?
In misty dreams of fame
Zebedee your father
Must miss you at the lake
His nets are daily tended
By no sons for profit's sake
The Nazarene is now your Rabbi and
Has captured your intent
Your will is yours but now you find it's
To you your Master lent
Boanerges, Boanerges
Ride Thunder to the brink
Baptizing self in giving up
A bloody cup you'll drink

FUTURES BRIGHT AND BOLD

Gotta let it go
Put it all to bed
Treat the haunting stories old
Like old friends that are dead

Make the things that've come to light
As fuel to be burned
Grasp the hope of better days
And let the past be spurned

Fear the avalanche of doubt
And run from drifting thought
Hold to current love and trust
The Maiden I have caught

Chance to lose the anchoring
From days now reminisced
Reach for futures bright and bold
And with this hope be kissed

Dinosaur Tracks

Underneath the dinosaur
Are footprints leading there
Leading to the place we long
To see some visions rare

Like the rainbow's golden end
It's hard to really find
But setting off to journey there
Is candy for the mind

Was it drought or comet gas?
That chased him from the earth
Or was it you and me who came?
At dawn of mankind's birth

They say our feet walked not the path
Of simultaneous search
We did not see the wind blown trees
From co-existent perch

Who knows for sure if footprints crossed?
To quench a primitive thirst
Who knows if we saw Godly clues?
Or if dinosaurs saw them first

Wonder long or wonder short
Or wonder as you choose
And look for footprints in the mud
But first take off your shoes

On That Day

On that day, some will be lifted
Some will discover what they really believe
When it arrives, the lost will be gifted
With the knowledge that loved ones have taken their leave

On that day the sky will break open
Invisible to some, but for those who are gone
After it's here, some will be hoping
That the voice of their longing will somehow be wrong

On that day, the saved will be gathered
And dark cold blindness will give way to thaw
With His blood, their souls have been lathered
And faith will take substance in trumpeting awe

On that day a great shout will hearken
Throughout all the heavens will go forth a call
And suddenly then, will come Light to the darkened
And change will awaken the great and the small

On that day, the end will be starting
A small girl will wonder why Mommy's not here
On that day a husband will whisper
"I think she was right," as he looks in the mirror

On that day the world will be reeling
But then return to its peaceful content
One will explain that the loved ones are feeling
The wrath of the answer that God has just sent

On that day, the Lord will diminish
The doubt that frankly imprisoned us all
Perhaps again, He'll say, "It is finished"
As He pulls us by hand from a terrible Fall

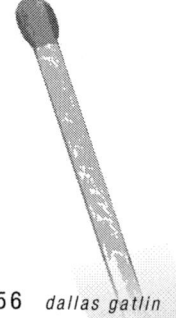

Honestly

Call it what you will
Call it love
Call it infatuation
Call it affirmation if you think you need to
But know what it means to you, honestly

See me how you will
See me friendly
See me attractive
See me supportive of all that is you
But know how to see me full, honestly

Hold me how you will
Hold me tightly
Hold me for protection
Hold me loving what I do for you
But know who is holding you, honestly

Love me if you will
Love me rightly
Love me for no reason but a decision that you do
Love me even when I don't now, seem to love you
But know who it is, who really loves you, honestly

My Pearls

Days long past
Remind us of
A sweet dependence
An endless love

Four great kids
Some leaving home
It's our great story
A precious tome

To teach, to work?
Nate thought real long
Two great life missions
None right, or wrong

To run, to run
Nic's heart and soul
To psych, to psych
His noble goal

Out east, out west
Em's all grown up
She's found her niche
Yup, yup, yup, yup

To learn, to learn
Ty's current passion
He's one right angle
With "big hair" fashion

To love, to live
Our life-long trip
A few little stumbles
But who gives a rip

We've got it all
Forged by our God
Who made my mind
And made your bod

Three billion women
All wanting this man
But only one Baby-Face
Can squeeze this hand

So shout it loud
Of all the girls
You're the one
Who holds my pearls

The Candle's Burning

The candle's burning, see it melt?
It seems no change in warmth is felt
No reason to worry, or feel afraid
The world I think for me was made

One day to wake is like another
No need to walk beside each other
I love to watch the day go by
Another waits, hello, good-bye

The sky will stretch out dawn 'til dusk
The corn will shed its gilded husk
The bird will chase the butterfly
And I will watch as both go by

Look now for night seems come to stay
I didn't plan to come this way
The darkness has changed from last time here
My careless peace seems turned to fear

I wonder why I hadn't seen
The way for others, life has been
There's nothing new come with the sun
When last days visit, for Adam's son

For substance, hope my mind inclines
With death and life the butler dines
The evidence of murders past
Of faith not seen, of life that lasts

SHIVERING

Shivering, wondering if daylight will ever come
Thinking about all the things that I've said and what I may have done
Wondering if the life I've lived can save me from being discarded
Hoping that it's not my only hope when I'm a "dearly departed"

Noting that no one I've known, has really known for sure
Counting on a borrowed truth, now only seen in blur
Wondering if it's strong enough to wrest me from this place
Yearning for a lucky draw that throws my way an ace

Caring not that minutes pass, or where they go or how
Knowing that great darkness sits just moments from this now
Wondering if my consciousness of me is truly mine
Challenging the notion that the end is something fine

Courting now the lady who can softly sing my name
Saving all the moments lost to hope for gentle fame
Wondering now if what I've lost is all that big a deal
Counting on a grace not mine since nothing seems for real

One Short Life

Frozen fingers licked of life
Frost loved toes kissed by a knife
Nostrils flared and then collapsed
A white flag raised, an anthem gasped

What has happened, how did it pass?
One short life and ebbing fast
So many things now left undone
What will be said of me, anon?

A gray fog settles around my head
These legs not mine, like frozen lead
More peaceful than I ever thought
I wonder what my life has wrought

RESCUE DAMNED

Flight of fancy
Slight of hand
Exploring futures
Probes unmanned

Rite of passage
Might have planned
Restoring virtues
Thinking banned

Night of torment
Blighted land
Imploring vestures
Music canned

Quite the finish
Sinking sand
Detouring gestures
Rescue damned

Just Fooling

Luck, Fate, Blessing
Chance, Grace, Confessing
Step, Fall, Regressing
Light, Life, just Guessing

Sin, Slip, Cooling
Spirit, Soul, Ghouling
Sip, Lap, Drooling
Death, Sleep, just Fooling

Luck, Slip, just Guessing
Chance, Sleep, Confessing
Step, Grace, Drooling
Death, Life, just Fooling

Rapture Day

The trumpet sounds and now we know,
The day for long we waited so!
The time was short, but I don't care,
Elation quickly fills the air!
My buoyant self seems strangely well,
No pain, no hurt, no fear to quell!
Just air and light beneath my feet,
And I'm not falling for sake of Pete!
And as I look around and fly,
A vast new army fills the sky!
All laughing lovely, while faces glow,
With arms raised up just like they know!
That God has kept a promise made,
I see Him now, as old things fade.
And all my doubts are washed away
It's now, it's here, it's Rapture Day!

When Adam Sinned

When Adam sinned, right after Eve
He asked I Am to take His leave
No longer lord of God's creation
He deeded to Satan his rightful station

To blame his wife was his first thought
After all she Satan's pitch had bought
But Adam listened to his wife
And for this deed, he lost his life

Oh not right then, for sure he breathed
And for no wife or child he grieved
Not yet at least, but something loomed
For Adam's carefree life was doomed

Now by the sweat of hand and brow
He dug for food with ox and plow
And bounced a young boy on his knees
A boy who'd soon be climbing trees

But then as mind and body grew
Another brother now made two
And strikes and blows by envy grasped
Left lifeblood spilt while brother gasped

So Adam mourned for second son
And knew that death was finally come
And Satan laughed inside his head
That Abel Adam's son was dead

Then nature groaned to see the sight
The sun kissed days had turned to night
And weeds popped up in gardens groomed
While earth its once new friends entombed

When Adam sinned our lives all changed
Before we come, we're now estranged
From God the Granter of each choice
From His soft touch and gentle voice

Who can re-bridge, this bridgeless gap?
Who can this tangled mess unwrap?
Who but the One who made us thus,
Can Adam's sin undo for us?

Brood of Vipers

Brood of vipers
Two-time sons of smoking Hell
Cast your crowns of self-made hype
At the feet of someone well

Unwind the blood-soaked, lifeless ropes
You braid in willing prisoners' hair
Unbind the face of false consuming rash
With hands of trembling care

Clean the dish from inside out
Make your sin-stained temple pure
Wash your hands in mercy's fount
Purge your whitewashed sepulcher

Blood of Abel, surely stored
Dead men's bones to soak
A jealous temple trampling Lord
Their law-to-self revoke

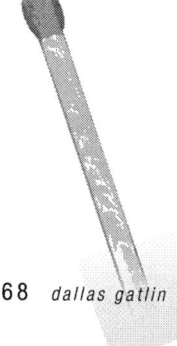

Woe to you, you legless snake
No chance your law will heal
The wounds your words and deeds inflict
And fates your teachings seal

A tenth of this, a tenth of that
But justice finds no home
And faithfulness and mercy die
Still-born in righteous Rome

Jerusalem, Jerusalem
How long will you not see
The Love that gathers seekers safe
To safety that is free

Children come, and learn of Me
Grab hold, I'll lift you out
Listen to the Voice that calls
Let faith defeat your doubt

With Your Maker Dance

Capture the beauty
Of sunlit greens leaves moving to a cold, cutting wind
Sense the song they sing as they dance
Let the chorus and the harmony
That comes together without effort
Engulf you in a glorious peaceful trance

Capture the majesty
Of the One who knows your worries can be shed
If even for a moment in a God sent holy trance
Helpless like a ballet dancer in a light and graceful lift
And set upon a tranquil plateau where you can whirl and sing
And in lockstep rhythm, leap for joy and with your Maker dance

THE MISSIVE

The missive came without invitation
Folded as if with care reserved
For a prized possession
It arrived like a raven tapping
And ravished my heart
As a meal

The mystery missive appeared
As if created from nothing
Prompted by a need to exist
It arrived like a rabid dog
Drinking the life
From my bones

The unasked for missive took aim
Took aim at my arrogant settled-ness
In loving my beloved too tamely
It drenched my dryness with jealousy's oil
Stoking the fire
That had nearly gone out

The missive haunts me even now
Like a stain unmoved by effort
It lives at the door of my days
Like a raven tapping
Tapping a missive, tapping
Reminding me to attend

I Am Lost

I am lost
I know not what
The past can offer
To ease the pain

Once it's done
It's all locked in
I can contemplate
But what's to gain

I cannot change
The things that were
By force of will
To change its truth

Though try I might
By logic's sword
It's what it is
There's changeless proof

You Fill My Hollow

The wonder of it latches tight
To hold my lonely heart tonight
It keeps me focused
Keeps me sane
Hugs my hollow, empty pain
And makes it warm
Instead of cold
Replacing hurt
With love to hold
The wonder of you comes just right
To fill my lonely heart tonight
A place that's shaped
For only you
You fill my hollow that you do

The Chase

"OK," I said, "I'll go outside"
And in the sun and wind confide
She bid me get to know the birds,
"They speak with movement, not with words"

I chased some for a little while
Their movements spoke with grace and style
With every flit and every flight
I thought I could, I thought I might

Be able to, reach out and grasp
Some tail feathers and then alas
One little creature, would be mine
To loose and catch another time

"And then", I said, "I'll go o'er there"
And catch a bee right from the air
I'll hold her gently until she sees
I have no sting, just need to please

A natural push that seems a chase
Can pleasure best at slower pace
So overtaking's not the goal
But merging sweetly, soul to soul

"OK," I said, "I'll go inside,
And in your warm embrace confide"
She bid me, "Chase the bees and birds,
Speak now with movement, not with words"

Twelve Men

Twelve men, walking,
        -listening, watching
Twelve men, hearing,
        -hoping, laughing
Twelve men, working,
        -doing, helping
Twelve men, eating
        -hearing, wondering
Twelve men, responding,
        -fearing, doubting
        -running, betraying
Twelve men, alone,
        -dying, living

PLANKS

The planks swing
    no edges discerned
Except as they swing
    except as they swing
Each moves me forward
    to nothing at all
Except to the end
    except to the end
The Rhythm's the same
    always the same
Each step is in time
    each step is in time
The planks swing
    as white as can be
It's all white the same
    it's all white the same
Each step is in time
    always in time
The gaps are the same
    so white and the same
Eternity wide
    ever so wide
No beginning or end
    beginning or end
Each step moves me forward
    be careful don't fall
And walk to the end
    just walk to the end

Light Years from Earth

Light years from earth, in some place and time
Spins another, wonderful, world sublime
It teems with life and sub-consciousness
Of its own sense of being
And its own traffic mess

Miles and miles above us or down
Moves some other rush hour, in some bustling town
It moves with a purpose all of its own
With subconscious creatures
All headed for home

Even farther out somewhere, lives One who observes
Each one of our lane changes, all of our swerves
One with a purpose who speaks like a mime
With His own sense of being
His own sense of time

But maybe much closer, is He to us all
Than we can imagine, on this here blue ball
He's neither far out there, nor watching from stars
But sitting beside us
Right here in our cars

And light years from earth, in some other place
I wonder if others are tracking our race
I wonder if drivers swerve left and then right
With Him sitting side them
In traffic at night

An Un-gelded Sailor

Golden rocks near golden shores
Glistening sailors stowing oars
Gliding in toward spear-like reefs
Glancing blows from courage thieves

Guiding nerves o'er creaking decks
Gaping rocks hold ancient wrecks
Gallant sailors came this way
Gerent voyagers game to play

Gaunt and girded in his loins a
Gelded sailor stoic joins
Goaded by the fear of quitting
Gutting fear with each new shitting

Gamer he, who knows no stopping
Granting life to those who're dropping
Guillotined of anxious waiting
Giving power to heads awaiting

Gone all cursed fear and sweating
Gone like tangled useless netting
Glistening faces holding strong
Good landing safe though night was long

Hand in Glove

More than my lover
Nola sweet lass
I love your smooth meadows
And your once conquered crevasse

More than my lady
My Nola undressed
I dream of your mountains
And their heavenward crests

More than my soul mate
Nola my love
I yearn for your closeness
My hand in your glove

A Moment in Paradise

Paradise was very close
I didn't know it then
I only new the tension sweet
That built as I came in

I drove to your house, half entranced
Mostly thinking of your hair
And seeing you just made it "worse"
When my eyes met your stare

I walked you to my car I know
But don't remember much
But I can smell your sweetness then
And I recall your touch

We drove to Paradise that day
And spoke of nonsense things
And listened as that Lady laid
And thought of thoughts that brings

We played and felt the tension build
Wondering if we had impressed
You thought of pure romantic things
I dreamed of you undressed

And finally to the Isle we strolled
Hands held with nervous joy
A girl scared, but longing to
Feel loved by that young boy

He knew somehow he'd kiss her
She knew he wanted to
He pulled her there down to the grass
Their lips now passion's glue

It was a moment in Paradise
Like nothing known before
Seems like we walked up to that place
And busted through the door

A moment in heaven to seal the deal
Of lovers meant for life
A young boy kissed his girl that day
He knew he'd found his wife

Young Love

Young Love, hearts waiting
Two souls, faith keeping
Loneliness, melancholy
Days unending
Beautiful weekends, soon over
Years passing

New Life! Hearts joining
Patience winning
Sunshine silhouette, hands clasping
Rings shining, love glowing, plans unfolding

Fears, Joy, Misunderstanding mingled
Temptation, confusion, commitment overcoming
Life and love growing
Blessings flowing
Children laughing, crying, hugging, growing

Young love. Still burning, hearts hurting
Two souls, faith keeping, God holding
Loneliness, melancholy
Misunderstandings pervading

The Letter, unwanted visitor, ghosts haunting
God driving, Light Shining, Faith sustaining
Love winning

Young love, hearts joining
Two souls, faith keeping
Passion renewed, Love blazing, hope raising
Faith certain, devotion unquestioned, love endless
Memories precious, future boundless
Young Love

Green Eyes Lovely

Green eyes lovely
Full of grace
Brown eyes smile to see her face
Precious moment, full of wonder
Long locks gently held in lace

Brown eyes valiant
Looking south
Strong heart longs to kiss her mouth
Anxious moment, full of waiting
One short walk, one life, one vow

Brown eyes, Green Eyes
Piercing fire
Passion leads our private choir
Eternal moment, full of love
A six-year journey of faith, desire

Green eyes, Brown eyes
Mating souls
Coming from such different poles
Pregnant moment, full of wonder
One love, one heart, one set of goals

Green eyes lovely
Brown eyes valiant
Princess faithful, Steed is gallant
Royal moment, full of splendor
She rides off on her white stallion

How About Me and Then You

The Serpent beguiled the woman to eat
The man came right along side
Found joy for a minute, but then it was gone
Down deep it felt like they died

The earth and the heavens, too felt the pain
Groaning as if they were ill
The darkness that came fell down like a cloak
And all of creation stood still

Leviathan sleeps in the dust of the earth
Where oceans had played and convulsed
Behemoth thundered his presence in all
Vibrations of fear in each pulse

The man and the woman ran off to a place
The shame nipping fast at their heals
But they could not hide, from their darkness inside
As they longed for the Light that reveals

Silly it seems, to hide from the Light
That sees everything that we do
Adam and Eve came back from the Night
How about me; and then you?

Djellaba

Djellaba
All dressed up in pomp
Circumstances calling for a hidden gate
Walking quickly
Pretending to be about some important matter
Check under your hood why don't you?
You power yourself with a mystic fuel
Fuel you share with no one else
Your robe, it hides your girth
You who feeds yourself by taking in puffs
Of praise offered up to your apparent holiness
When the whole of you amounts to no more
Than Oz's wizard

Djellaba
Undress yourself of pomp
Circumscribe your life and find the hidden gate
Walking honestly
Set about some truly important matter
Let down your backward pulled up hood
Unmask the mystic fog that shrouds your future
Share with us what you see at every forward step
Your robe; let it drop to show your worth
You'll find you need this garb much less than you think
So strip away the comfort of praises undeserved
And see the holy whole of you
And stomp the lizard

A Comitia of Two

Comitia, that's what we need
Let's get it all out in the open
Shout it from the top of a stone tower
As they cheer and amen
Let the affirmation of our words bring us power

Assemble, get all our opponents together
That's what we'll do
And take their logic apart word by word
Like a puzzle or riddle
Then scatter their flock skyward, each a confounded bird

Comitia, just you and me now
On top of our game
Shout it from the top of our conquered perch
A king and a queen
Basking in the glory of a lifelong search

The Poet Died

Truth elusive
Stories told
Pieces fitted
New and old
Tales shared
And legends saved
Details slipping
Castles caved
Secrets hidden
Someone lied
Peace forbidden
The Poet died

The Poet Lives

Truth restores a wounded heart
A window that reveals
The hidden things that haunt the day
And slowly, surely heals

Truth cements a solid house
A binding that is strong
The stones that build a shelter from
The things that we did wrong

Truth provides a peaceful place
A haven that forgives
A resurrection from sure death
And now the Poet lives

The Resurrection

It happened one winter
A deep, long fall
From grace, from light, from you
A sudden suspension
From all that I knew
From peace, from love, from you
It happened so quickly
At least so it seemed
To me, now lost, from you
A sudden replacement
A deep, long fall
From grace, from light, from you
It happened to reach me
To find you in view
To see you so purple, and new
A sudden resurrection
From death in my pew
To grace, to life, to you

Last Place in a Fast Race

They work, they labor, they run to finish
Get lapped because of their pace
Some snicker, some clap, some just lower their eyes
To avoid the slow runner's face

Four hundred lined up, and left at the gun
Some sprinted to reach the narrow trail
The leaders looked strong, as their lean legs stretched long
The rest snaked behind like a tail

As the evening race flew, and the energy grew
All the people cheered loud in delight
And as the strong finished, the pack now diminished
Each one drew applause here tonight

They cheered, then they walked, quickly off to their boys
Each father and mother so proud
The last boy runs on, his plodding legs done
Alone now and dodging the crowd

Three hundred yards more and each stride a chore
His courage just lights up his face
Some snickered, some clapped, some lowered their eyes
But none of them finished the race

Why the Whining?

Cancel the picnic
The ants are marching
The wind is gusting
And the sun is scorching
The mosquitoes have found us
And the salad is wilting
Cancel the picnic and go home

Call off the party
A storm is coming
Our friends are busy
And the neighbors are fuming
The hornets have found us
And the chips have crumbled
Cancel the party and go home

Forget the concert
The rain is threatening
The band is tardy
And the wind is deafening
The black flies have found us
And the seats are like granite
Cancel the concert and go home

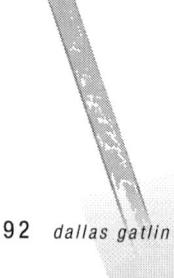

dallas gatlin

Stop all the breathing
It's all too much effort
The pulse is monotonous
And it's not clear what we're here for
The buzzards have found us
And the days are like centuries
Stop all the breathing and go home

Cancel the whining
The ants are marching
Our friends are busy
And the wind is deafening
The buzzards have found us
And they're not all that hungry
So cancel the whining and go on

I Love the Rain

I love the rain
It reminds me of you
I love the way it makes me come inside

I love the rain
It refreshes like you
I love the way it let's me get wet then dried

I love the rain
It provides like you
I love the way it makes me grow

I love the rain
It cleanses like you
I love the way it makes me new, you know?

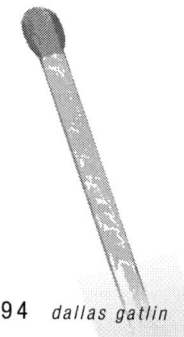

Like Windmills

Our windmill stands to remind us
That not everything needed is seen
It moves to invisible streams of power
A willing and grateful machine

It stands with its blades held out forward
And catching its strength from the sky
Its trinity feet planted firm in the earth
And its fingers attempting to fly

It transfers its power to our toiling
And provides meaningful, helpful assist
But in truth, we should be like the windmills
And by heavenly power be kissed

Heartless Mountain

Krakatoa, east of Java
What a sight it must have been
So long looking calm and placid
Sudden judgment bursts the Zen

How can a mountain care so little?
About the people down below-
When they live there so contented
Knowing not their coming woe

't would be nice to think her angry
With some malice for their souls
When she killed them with her fury
Poured out wrath in molten bowls

If at least it was intention
Some inherit worth implied
But since she did it so uncaring
't was all in vain that day they died

ALON

Alon and alas
She captures the world
Alon she endures

Alon is my love
She lets down her hair
In castles of gold, Alon

Alon and always
She conquers my thoughts
Alon she endures

Alon is my heart
She laughs with her eyes
Her eyes of cool green, Alon

Alon and away
She flies near my wings
Alon she endures

Alon is my life
She lives to love me
And me to love her, Alon

Enough

No time to waste
Worrying
No apologies
Too tough
No need for haste
Hurrying
No road, no way
Too rough
No proof to taste
Currying
Your love today
Enough

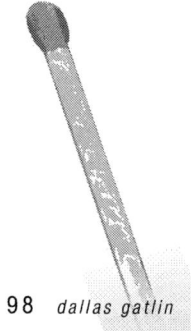

First Kisses

There were some kisses not a few
There were so many not shared with you
But all have faded with passing time
Now all I remember are yours and mine

There were some kisses some might call "first"
But there are no memories to put in verse
Gone they are like passing mist
And all I treasure, is when first *we* kissed

John's Pass

Blue and reddish orange ablaze
Above the calm and docile waves
The sun is tired and so are we
God's peace descends on you and me

Now over the gulf the cloudless sky
Is filled with pelicans soaring by
And coming low to scoop their prize
With folded wings and focused eyes

The dolphins surface playing school
Teachers, students in nature's pool
I wonder what they're thinking now
Are we in their thoughts today somehow?

Screaming gulls have checked the time
As fishing boats sail in, in line
And dock to barter this day's catch
The anxious gulls inspect each batch

At Gator's people sit and talk
While others stroll the boarded walk
At Scully's lines begin to form
The air is salty, moist, and warm

And at John's Pass the day now ends
For Dolphins, birds, and human friends
And all God's creatures breathe a sigh
As day is done and night draws nigh

Joy of My Life

You are the Joy of my Life

The Fire in my heart

The Rhythm of my Days

The Hope in my Dreams

You are the Mother of my children

Their Source, with God and Me

Living Lightly

Bearings only partly known
Scanning for the sun
Fearing clouds, and mist, and trees
On a suicidal run

I could have had a course mapped out
A compass to consult
I could have stopped when first I sensed
A coming bad result

But now I must resolve myself
To focus like ne'er before
And shoot through each new opening
Like a swiftly closing door

No time to fear a mistaken choice
No energy to spare
I must fight off the fear and doubt
And fly from here to there

It's kind of freeing in a way
To look at things this tightly
And cast away old paralyses
By traveling this path lightly

A Persistent Suitor

Life is a wonder
A gift of travel
Down a winding rural road
Sun, peaking in and out of leaves

Life is a wandering hike
A precarious walk
Across a swiftly flowing stream
Barefoot, rock to slippery rock

Life is a good book
A magnetic read
Pulling us ever forward into its plot
Pages turning, with not much thought for the end

Life is a picnic
A feast of flavors
Sweet, sour, bitter casual courses
A tablecloth, readied for the next guests

Life is tomorrow
An optimistic ride
Across a swiftly flowing ether
Sun rising, setting . . . and rising again to new faces

Life is courage
A stoic fight
Against a stronger foe
A melancholy surrender to a persistent suitor

The Skeptic's Sip

The skeptic wondered 'loud to me
And challenged me to tell him
Tell the reason for my hope
The reason for my rest

I rest from certain doubts I hold
And hold to things unseen
"You trust in things invisible-
Is that your very best?"

"So do you," I said to him
"You value things not seen-
Like love, and law, and loyalty-
The wind that moves the trees"

"Indeed I do," he said to me,
"But God's another thing-
I want to think that if He's there
He'd thaw my spirits freeze"

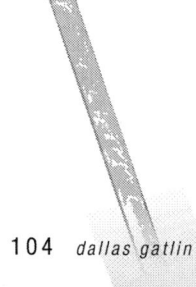

"Oh thaw He will if you come close-
To melt your skeptic's heart
He'll answer questions; all you have
With more than you'd have guessed"

"He'll judge you first and this you'll feel—
With sadness, fear, remorse—
But then He'll come and visit you
With peace, and grace, and rest"

"So come, please come, and drop your hands
And reach out now for His
And clasp them; feel them with your own
And see where they were ripped"

"I think I feel, His palms, they're warm"—
My skeptic said aloud
"I think I see the evidence—
I taste what you have sipped"

Curled Under All Around

Cuddled up
And cuddled down
Curled under all around

Snuggled in
And snuggled close
Hugged-up tight in double dose

Merging in
And then back out
With each merge a primal shout

Coming through
And coming by
With each coming, comes a sigh

Gazing deep
And gazing long
All quite right and nothing wrong

Sleeping with
And sleeping sound
Curled under all around

Not Enough Rhyme

Too many seconds
Not enough time
Too many poems and
Not enough rhyme
Too many rhythms
Not keeping time
Too many words said
Not enough mime
Too many buzzers
Not enough chime
Too many oranges
Not enough lime
Too many tea leaves
Not enough thyme
Too many poems writ
Not enough rhyme

Death, I Smile

Death, I smile at you
You are such a pittance
Unable to block my admittance
To a room prepared for me

You can no more hold me in the grave
Than I can hold the wind in my hand
You sting, yes, but only for a moment
You pismire to which I grant more than you're due

Death, I wave at you
You are a joke
Just a neglected Coke
Now absent of its fizz

Death, I smile at you
I laugh a careful laugh
Sleep with one eye open half
Waiting for that day

A VIOLET HUE

A violet hue ties me to you
A cord from young heart to heart
A violet hue runs from our "I do"
To a wonderful, magical start

A violet perfume adrift on the leaves
Loved filled thoughts of those days
When violet lilacs could travel the breeze
And turn Aprils, to life giving Mays

A violet blanket rests on your skin
While love takes on a new look
When violet colors write something again
In Nola's and Dallas's book

Homemade Chains

Please ignore these homemade chains
That run between my feet
Please excuse my stumbling gate
As I lean to take a seat

Please do not be angry
At the anger I express
Please forgive my rambling thoughts
As I sort through all this mess

I cannot change the things I've done
Nor can you do the same
I can only look upon these chains
And absorb most of the blame

I do not want to make you sad
Or imprison you in grief
In truth I want to free you from
The jail of false belief

But my motives are not purely good
They're selfish in some ways
Yet from these chains I must escape
Self-pity never pays

Chancy the Cat

Chancy is black, black as the night
A furry defender of all that's cat right
Hiding from monsters and fearing each noise
She trusts no adults, no girls, and no boys

But now and again, when she needs a cool drink
She'll appear from the shadows and leap to the sink
Lapping with gusto, till her thirst is quite quenched
Her paws are all wet and her whiskers are drenched

Then on occasion, when needing some love
She'll show up from nowhere and give you a nudge
One measured moment of tipping her hat
These are our memories of Chancy the cat

A Phrase Rings

A phrase rings round my head today
It dances to some tunes
Tunes that change and come and go
And move like shifting dunes

But yet the words themselves, you know
Stay pretty much the same
As those that visited my mind
Since first I knew my name

As I lay softly in my crib
'Twas two or maybe three
And wondered 'bout the world out there
And how it came to be

"Who am I?" rang the phrase out then
"Who am I?" to the tune
The words just danced with wonder then
Like sand in shifting dune

The phrase still rings around my head
It dances to a song
A song that now has taken shape
With lyrics I've known long

The tune has now become well known
All others set aside
"Who am I?" still the words ring out
As most my friends have died

With tune well set, I sing my song
While lying in my bed
Who I am will soon be clear
The shifting sands have said

A Martingale

It would not be a martingale
To hold your focus tight
It should not be a martingale
To keep your mind from flight
Fast to your girth
And from our birth
I want your faith
For what it's worth
It's worth a million words to me
To have you here but have you free
So it should not take a martingale
To keep your thoughts on me

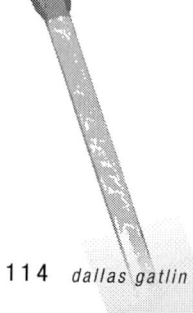

A Plaited Omnipotent Love

You pleach my strands with yours
Braided hopes, and braided motives
Decorate the very glory of our heads
Plaiting gold and silver, platinum and stone
Pliable lives as if the unchangeable
Could be gently bent and coaxed without pain
To form a common lock

You teach my strands to bend
Woven straw, patterned grasses
Form the very beauty of our lives
Weaving hemp and reeds, scarlet and string
Pliable strands of history merged as if
Two very different families could be glued without breaking
To form an omnipotent love

Can it Be?

Can it be I found the perfect mate?
Can it be that no other lock can hold the key
That lives inside my heart?

So young with so much time ahead
So sure of something so suddenly arrived
So ready to commit

Can it be I found the lovely one?
The beauty missing from the grayness of my soul;
To cure the hollow ache

So innocent she lays upon the grass
So sure that I will not invade her now
So ready to commit

Can it be I found the peace to tame my inner fire?
Can it be no other one can capture my desire?
Has the answer fallen in my lap?

So free her smile calls to me
So sweet her lips she gives for free
So ready to commit to me

Dance in the House by the Hill

Razor sharp, your words cut right through
Muscle, and nerve, and new manly sinew
For a moment my heart yearns to genuflect
As I measure retort with quick circumspect

Why not, just nod and say you agree
Why not, say something real nice about me
But no, you give me just what I deserve
No flattery tossed and it's still your serve

To think, I've been thinking only of me
To hold, to less than I really could be
And fabricate fables as I sometimes do
When I could strip naked and share life with you

I think, that maybe I'll just take a chance
To tell you my real name, then ask you to dance
And then if you hold me and say that you will
We'll dance until midnight, in the house by the hill

My Teacher's Words

It isn't oft you catch me
Nodding off this way
It doesn't seem to be enough
Your voice my mind to sway

But when my eyes begin to cross
And it seems I'm far away
Just remember I hear your words
For in my dreams they play

Your Face a Song

As I drive away, please know that you'll stay
In your own special private place
I'm leaving you now, but will keep you somehow
Even as I leave for the chase

I'm leaving with you, the knowledge anew that
You live in your own secure place
I'm taking along, a lovely song
In the notes that trace out your face

Fly with You

It's a beautiful day
There's so much to do
I breathe, I drink
I walk with you
I taste, I see
I think aloud
I boast; I fall
I'm humble, proud
It's a beautiful day
It's sunny blue
Above gray clouds
I fly with you

In Our Garden

The windmill makes a silent hum
I hear it with my eyes
The sunflowers pull the bees to them
To try them on for size
As clouds make pillows for the birds
To dart both in and out
The sun makes shadows of us all
It's fun to think about
My dearest stands here with me
Joined now hand to hand
And mind to mind we're dancing here
God's love our wedding band

Sapphire Star

Sapphire star
Redeemed with great price
Knocked from its orbit
Not once, but twice

Sapphire star
Hidden from view
Its light covered over
As if we were through

Sapphire star
An orphan again
Sent to bed hungry
To fool an old friend

Sapphire star
Red box made its home
A gift from its nemesis
He couldn't have known

Sapphire star
Now missed for its love
Its certainty, passion
For hope, quite enough

Sapphire star
Restored to its place
It's gold radiant orbit
Out shining in space

Sapphire star
All purplish-blue
A comet-like message from
Your me, to my you

Wonder What the Fairness Is?

Wonder what the fairness is, wonder at the words
Cringe at all the wounds that come from sharpened verbal swords

Armored round the neck and heart
Shield held fast and tight
Knife tucked deep inside my belt
Per chance I have to fight

Wonder what the fairness is, wonder at the praise
Sting from all the truth found out, pulled back from former days

Fortress round the heart, the soul
Built up gray stone by stone
Oil waits, green caldrons hot
To scorch them to the bone

Wonder what the fairness is; wonder for right now
Cower from my own defense, my careless, senseless vow

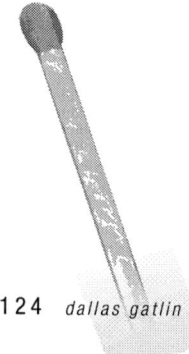

While the Cicadas Sleep

While the cicadas sleep
Friends become lovers
And lovers lie down
Then lie to each other
They share of their dreaming
Both shallow and deep
And tire of the toiling
While the cicadas sleep

While the cicadas sleep
Some prey and then kill
Pretending communion
Till lifeless and still
Taking what's priceless
Declaring it cheap
Awakening judgment
While the cicadas sleep

It seems we've been dozing
While predators roam
Gestating in earth wombs
But turning to bone
Sown to be living
Our maker to reap
Instead we are rotting
While the cicadas sleep

The Stranger's Lair

Couldn't you see the trend?
Wasn't it easy to just pretend?
Far be it from her to sense the end
That lay at the feet of a stranger's friend

Why did you decide to wait?
How did you miss the signs of fate?
Far be it from her to get there late
And stray down the path to the stranger's bait

Have you now given the whole thing up?
Can't you this inertia simply interrupt?
Far be it from her to see the snare
That waits for her now in the stranger's lair

Shouldn't you check the time of day?
"Isn't it later than six?" you say
Far be it from her to know the time
As she waits for the stranger to sit and dine

Won't you wonder if this course is right?
Haven't you considered this could be your night?
Far be it from her to see it now
As she looks for the stranger to love her somehow

The Voice

Irritating nuisance making God forsaking noise
Amusement taking, gladness faking, sick-leave taking toys
Looking happy, talking sappy, dancing rappy boys
Brave looking, travel booking, manufactured poise
Can't see through it, shouldn't do it, conscience bomb deploys
Hiding sissies, pregnant missies, primping dead decoys
Gave no answer, Donner, Prancer, dashing man-made joys
All too quickly Santa's sickly leaving us no choice
Angels turn to, see us burn through, elementary ploys
Questions kill us, answers fill us, let us now rejoice
Finally, our eyes can see, our ears can hear the Voice
Calling Presence, to my essence, cutting through the noise

The Solitary Vase

It sits upon the table lone
A vase of royal color
It holds the nectar
To be sure of
Two flowers
That are lovers
A table too
Sits solitaire
And holds this life
In place
Four little cattails
Play below
Their home
Is in the vase
Together there
They've made a life
Invisible to most
But life it is
Both full and sweet
With God
Their solid host
Close to the edge
They find their lot
But safe all
Just the same
And stand to show
Those who care to see
That life is
In His Name

Saints' Hopeful Gaze

Saints sit by on hills and wait
In sunlit, shadowless days
They wait for friends who've also seen
Through faith's new hopeful gaze

And saints walk free through forests green
Through leaves that ne'er fall
By trees whose branches never twist
With bark that makes no gall

They walk and sing and speak with praise
Towards the one who gives them life
And talk of days that soon will be
When husband rejoins wife

The saints embrace a family tie
That binds each soul to soul
Though marriage is not now what it was
There's love found in the whole

They all peer over an ether band
That lies between two planes
And hold to life like child to mother
Eternity remains

It's all a now to them but not
To us as we wait to see
What saints are watching from the hills
So held by God yet free

Rainbow's Breeze

Copper colors
Golden leaves
Yellows, oranges
Rainbow's breeze
Autumn aura
Sunlit days
Frosty mornings
Dusk conveys
A coming quiet
Frozen air
Biting winds
And branches bare
Hiding critters
Huddling friends
Finding warmth
'Til this one ends
And shivering darkness
Gives way to blues
Those copper colors
Nature's hues
When golden sunrise and
Teal new leaves
Burst forth with fingers
In Rainbow's breeze

Then and Now

Mark the day I met you fine
Treat it as the start of time
Seal it with a smile, a wink
Write it down with violet ink

Cast your memories back to then
Leave today and go back when
Your love for me was just a thought
My love for you brand new, just caught

Think of things that we know now
Dream of dreams of *who*, not how
For you're the one from whom I draw
The love my dreams once only saw

But now I lift you with my soul
My heart leaps over the daisy knoll
And when I think of *who*, not how
You're in my dreams both then and now

My Flower

Hours
Flowers made of minutes
Blessed petals
Petals formed from thoughts
Each second, thoughts of you
Seconds come and go
Like breathing
With each breath
I take you in
And let you go again
Giving back
What I've enjoyed
If but for a second
My Flower

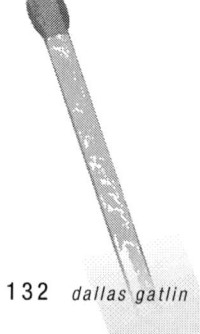

NATHANAEL

He found me, He found me
Beneath this here tree
How did He know me?
How did He see?

The name I was given
Nathanael, it's true
Within me is kindness
I've felt it since two

First born of my siblings
I'm called on to lead
And sometimes I stumble
Look, see my knees bleed?

But up I must get
And walk down the way
That leads to adventure
I must go today

All those that know me
Are scratching their heads
"Why not just stay here….
With warm quilts and beds?"

But I'll walk on with kindness
Not looking for fame
My name is Nathanael
And He knows my name

николь-dime

Heartbeat slow, heartbeat fast
Seems like days and days had passed
But soon he showed his blonde-haired head
"What a beautiful boy!" his mama said

Home he came, to find his place
And from day one, the boy could race
Round and round the block he'd go
His doggie Bernie fast in tow

Pushing Bubba in a wagon
Blue jeans 'round his butt a saggin'
Come on home to get some lunch
Sandwich and some Hi-C punch

Then one day to Woodside Trail
Boats in flooded sandbox sail
J, and Matt, and Eric hide
While Nic and Andy count inside

Sunday morning, Fenton Road
Drawing portraits of some toad
Ninja Turtles soon take shape
Masks and belts but please no cape!

Golden years of play and school
Girls are gross while boys still rule
Riding bikes to Dairy Queen
Bellies fat and wallets lean

Tree-house forts and woodsy camps
Daredevil flights over curbs and ramps
Then one slight miscalculation
Bloody chin-bone laceration

Summer days and winter storms
Buddies left for girlie forms
Graduation soon so soon
Meets, and tests, and lunch at noon

Friends hello, and friends good-bye
Same to Nate, and Em, and Ty
Faith and family chart the course
And running 5K's like a horse

Olivet's a place to start
A place to study; belch, and fart
Their top runner from day one
No place to train so soon he's done

Grand Rapids bound one winter night
One lonely room, "man what a bite!"
One Nic-named boy all by himself
With books and TV on his shelf

Now it seems he's manly grown
With thoughts and plans all of his own
Still Claus he is, and for all time
He'll be our precious Nickel-dime

The Emily Rose

Intense
Passionate colored flower
Sensitive and subtle
Guarded but kind

Beautiful petals
Held out to God
A sturdy stem
Not easily picked

All garden dwellers
Defer to this,
Passionate flower
A rose in the mist

Ty

Not just a thinker
Not just a boy
It seems the whole universe-
Is often his toy

A dreamer, a doer
He works 'til it's done
To him it's all easy-
At least it's all fun!

His heart is like gold
He never gets riled
He calls it "success"—
When others have smiled

In him is goodness
As he asks "how" and "why"
Our young man of wonder
We call him "Ty"

Settle in Home

Castaway, castaway, castaway home
Travel the trade winds
Sailing alone

Travel so lightly, stripped to the bone
Travel the east winds
Leading toward home

Find the light swiftly, before the fog sets
Feel for the harbor
And pull in the nets

Search for your darling, she's reading this poem
Glide to your docking
And settle in home

Two Worlds Spinning

Conflict rages, fear prevails
Children stare and women wail
Nighttime falls with no relief
A mother births a child of grief

Hopeful people, whistling tunes
Heading off for cheery noons,
Working toward a lovely dinner
Off to bed a peaceful sinner

Worlds turning, spinning storms
One rejoices, the other mourns
One gets rain, to nurture life
The other drowns in turbid strife

SHARING SHERON

What a sister, full of life
Lifelong mission, Stanley's wife
Loving mother of four boys
She loved them dearly, despite their ploys

Grandma Sheron loved to make
Things she'd craft and things she'd bake
Not a room without stuff in it
Works of art from each spare minute

Stories long and stories short
Tales of folks of every sort
Tales of roosters, loose emus
Tales of her dogs eating shoes

Always first to place the call
Summer, winter, spring, and fall
She always had so much to say
I only wish she'd call today

The Christmas Bacchant

Morning brings a strange release
A frenzied, frantic farce
A celebration of sacrifice
An oddly fashioned faith device
A warming tonic made of ice
Where thoughts of God are sparse

Oh Bacchus you are clever
We love you more and more
Our Dionysian dance consumes us
And you laugh at our drunken snore
You laugh as we drink and snore

The day ends with a sigh at last
An empty, quiet roar
A cold and clammy residual
An oddly fashioned kid you'll
Sacrifice to a non-individual
To a god who himself is a boar

Oh Bacchus you are clever
We love you more and more
Our Dionysian dance consumes us
And you laugh at our drunken snore
You laugh as we drink and snore

A Tennessee Farm

The farm was heaven-
To a six-year-old boy
A place to make believe—
To live a whole life in one summer
A pleasant musty smell at night—
To set the whippoorwills whistling—
And mesmerize a young boy listening

The stream was paradise—
To a full-of-awe boy
A place to chase green snakes—
To live a whole life in one wading
A slippery fun smell between the toes—
To set small slimy feet prancing—
And make a little boy enjoy dancing

The pasture was a kingdom—
To a full-of-wonder boy
A place to reign over subjects—
To play king and send Rex for the cows
A powerful whole feeling of ruling for joy—
To set a course with care to inspire—
And light a little man's curious fire

The porch was home—
To a six-year-old boy
A place to talk that time with Grandpa—
To live a whole life with that man in a moment
A pleasant tobacco smell in his lyrical voice—
To set the wisdom of his words to musical christening—
And mesmerize a young boy listening

Sand Pebble Sabbath

Walk with me now
Our toes on the beach
Seeking the sunset
'Fore John's Pass we reach

Pelicans sweeping
From rainbow to wave
Dolphins swim hiding
With legend to save

The smell of the water
Not fresh, and not stale
Gives pungent delight
Like bitters in ale

Chance on a rising
Of the drawbridge at night
The wait not a hassle
But a timely delight

A light meal at Gator's
A talk by the rail
The wind sings of summertime
As lovers set sail

Walk with me closely
Now back on the street
Through dark little alleys
That hasten our feet

Thinking 'bout nothing
By the light of spring's moon
We'll sleep at the Sand Pebble
And wake about noon

An Island of Treasure
Our Easter retreat
A small place of Sabbath
With sand on our feet

The Scenarist

Line upon line
Word after word
Plotting a course as it were
To tell us a story
And weave us a tail
And leave us in stitches
On tour

A mask of a fellow
His paper is yellow
The plot has now thickened so much
To get out his story
His life is now whorey
As he sells his poor soul
For a crutch

And line after line
He casts out his life
To sell it for pennies to us
But we are not listening
To words he thinks glistening
So he takes the back seat on the bus

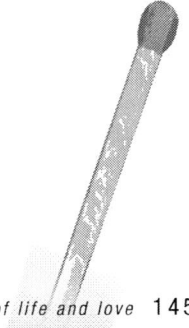

Nola My Passion

Love abounds with awesome splendor
From your Heart flows warm delight
Through your lips I taste you sweetly
Lying in my arms each night

Strands of hair caress my fingers
I capture you with strong embrace
With each breath my passion lingers
As my hands trace out your face

Leap my Heart, with great excitement
Searching for a place to rest
As my passion for you lingers
With each rising of your breasts

Burst my soul within you deeply
Making whole my half a life
Love from you is what completes me
I take anew my Bride, my wife

Never a Day

Never a day
That I do not need you
Never a minute that passes without
My heart longing to nurture and feed you
That is the mission God made me about

Never an hour
That I cannot see you
Never a second when your face disappears
My heart longing to hold and protect you
To cast into the ocean, every one of your fears

An Innocent Rebirth

Yesterday, a visit
To a place we've never been
A place we never thought we'd be
Can we go back again?

I can't explain the feeling
It's like a warm embrace
A longing to go in somewhere
And just enjoy the space

And when we finally got there
I knew it was all right
To just enjoy the being there
And maybe stay all night

The funny thing is finding it
You need someone to go
And walk you gently, step by step
Curiosity in tow

Yesterday, a discovery
A trembling in the earth
That started in your heart and mine
An innocent rebirth

POISON LEAVES

Poison leaves
To cover sins
Wear them, eat them
It now begins
Love me often
Leave me be
Write me, call me
Help me see
A different truth
Than lurks beneath
The clever stories
The poison wreath
Laugh and sing
With me, with him
Share your love
With cloven grin
Chase the guilt
That your heart cleaves
Forever eating
Poison leaves

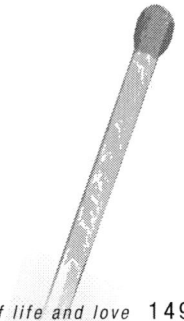

Violet Flowers

Violet flowers fell gently, cascading down your shapely waist
Encircled by chains of gold, shining like a radiant beacon cross
Illuminating my heart that day, with brave heart like intention
I made my plan and resolved to win the love I feared I'd lost

Your purple petals drew me, with royal irresistible delight
Captivating my darkened heart, with thoughts of my Princess saved
Holding my soul with golden chain, your love like magic retook me
A Prince, intent to carry his Princess, on golden roads he paved

THE OTHER SIDE

Look at the other side.
What is it you see?
Is it better, by far, than what you have?
Is it your dream?

Look at the time you have.
Can you count it?
Is it shorter, by far, than what you think?
Is it enough?

Look at the time of day.
Is it time?
Is this the hour of importance?
Can you tell?

Look at yourself in the mirror.
Do you know your name?
It is more honored than you know.
You are God's.

Nolita Oregano

I know a girl
Who has no idea
How important she is to spaghetti
A hardy girl, with minty lips
And both are moist and ready
A sprinkle of her
Can go a long way
To make a dish zesty and fine
An otherwise boring
And blandy ole pasta
Becomes a great reason to dine
Nolita Oregano sits at the table
Waiting for me to say grace
Waiting for me to pass her the sauce
And dab what she leaves on her face

Your Turn to Speak

It isn't the delicious taste
It isn't the intrigue
It isn't the capricious haste
It's more like good fatigue

It isn't the sensation sought
It isn't the delight
It isn't compensation's cost
It isn't that tonight

It isn't all the things you think
It isn't your last call
It isn't love nor is it lust
It's neither one at all

It isn't affirmation sought
It wouldn't sooth my need
It's not for rapt togetherness
It's not the nasty deed

It's only for a second dear
It's only you I seek
It's only words from your sweet lips
It's your turn now to speak

To Be Me

When I first knew I was me
I was on my back
Looking up as a
Veil-like sheer blew from the window
Toward an un-recalled but warm face
One I desired to lift me
Hold me
Me

When I first knew I was me
I was three
Looking ahead as a
Veil-like future blew in toward my face
A stained glass window, warm but undefined
One I desired to behold
Behold
Me

When I first knew I was me
I was new
Looking at my hands as a
Way to touch my face, my feet, my self
I recall a warmth, defined
One I desired to keep
To be
Me

On My Chiffonier

It sits there on the chiffonier
I see it sometimes clear
Some other times I don't at all
Nor do I hold it dear
It's neither wanted or despised
It's long past beauty faded, it
Cuts me to the marrow quick
And when it does it's hated
There's a secret there inside it
But not in velvet drawers
It's captured in the wood itself
It's seen in memories' auras
I've often thought of replacing it
Or crushing it for good
But it sits there on our chiffonier
I think I probably should
Its origin I don't recall
Yet sometimes it comes clear
Then it haunts me both with good and bad
Still on my chiffonier

The Whistling Wind

Listen to the wind
It whistles like it knows
It whistles like it knows I'm here
As it licks the fire that glows
The fire has nearly died tonight
It once was full and warm
It once was so dependable
It's orange inviting form
So sad to watch it fading
To sit here so alone
And feel the cold in only me
It chills me to the bone
What happens when the fire goes out?
The whistling wind responds
What happens when the smoke appears
And breaks these fragile bonds?
Listen to the wind tonight
It seems to call my name
It seems to sense I hear it too
As it extinguishes the flame

The Death Wish Squirrel

He who hesitates is lost
Said someone who thought he knew
But hesitation oft pays off
If you're not sure what to do

Take the squirrel that darts out in front
Of your car as you head down the street
Sometimes he stops, only to start
As your brain disengages your feet

What is he thinking when he shoots across
In front of your slow moving truck
Why he just now stopped and looked you in the eye
Is he despondent or just testing his luck?

Whatever it is; it's murder for you
Do you brake quickly or your steering wheel whirl
When you stand bumper to face, in the middle of the street
With a kamikaze-crazed death wish squirrel

A Spectator's Cage

Better to get, into the game
Than sit by the side of the court
Better by far to sail in a storm
Than to boast in a warm and safe port

Better to lose to an experienced foe
Than to talk about what you'd have done
Better to find vengeance through what you have learned
Than watch others have all of the fun

Better to live and risk all that you have
Than to sit by as others engage
Better to battle to win for a moment
Than to watch from a spectator's cage

Walking with You

Walking with you
Seems like dancing to a soothing mating rhythm
Walking by you
Seems like floating up near God and being with Him

Walking with you
I can feel the beat of nature's heart behind us
Walking by you
Seems there's nothing, and there's no-one who can find us

Walking with you
Feels like nothing matters more than listening to you
Walking by you
Feels as if the stars and sun are glistening through you

Walking with you
Takes the hurt and makes the fear here fail to beat us
Walking by you
Takes the power from all the things that could defeat us

You Wear My Ring

Every day now reminds me of spring
Every hour doth new wonderment bring
Every minute a new song to sing
Every moment that you wear my ring

Never again give thought to replace it
Never again with nakedness show
Never again lead stray thoughts to chase it
Never again from its home let it go

Every day now remember the spring
Every hour let new faithfulness bring
Every minute sweet new words to sing
Every moment that you wear my ring

A Zoo for You

Lucky duck
To be your man
Virile buck your biggest fan
Wagging dog
Right at your feet
Even there you smell so sweet
Your Cheshire cat
I crouch to spring
And to your lovely buttocks cling
A swimming fish
Inside your bowl
Yet hooking you remains my goal
A Silly goose
To talk like this
I'll just fly home and steal a kiss

Libeccio

Let Libeccio come, let it engulf me
Too long have I nested in this place
Let it come and warm me, take me
Let it guide my course to a different base

Willing sails set
Faith in the unseen
Substance dreamed of
I can see it

Let Libeccio come, let it carry me
So far that all the mud is left behind
Let it dry me out, and wet my taste for new
Re-set in me an adventurous mind

Careful courage abandoned
Hope in what can be
The unknown longed for
I must find it

Let Libeccio come, let it chase me
One gust behind a playful face
Let it try to catch me
Let it arrive in second place

Leave it to Me

Leave it to me
To keep you safe
Leave it to me to carry you off
Leave it to me to lay you down
In meadows cool, fragrant, and soft

Leave it to me
To hold your hand
Leave it to me to guide you true
Leave it to me to hold you up
And I will ever leave it to you

$E = MC^2$

$E=mc^2$
How can two protons be paired?
How can these forces
Like two harnessed horses
Be on one mission so intimately shared?

Neutrons taking up space
While electrons in tethered clouds race
Like planets? Not really
It's a statistical dealy
Not orbits in time or in place

Adam and Eve from clay
Another mysterious way
That God made from one thing
A beautiful something
A yes from an otherwise neigh

Saturday Morning

Saturday morning and I am in love
My world has been blessed with a princess
It's Saturday morning we went for a walk
She's captured my soul and my senses

Saturday morning, and she loves me too
Our world is so full of enchantment
It's Saturday morning and we just made love
God's most beautiful and gracious commandment

The Daily Push

I felt the push that bids me rise
But did not move a limb
I pictured myself getting up
But laid there foggy, dim

I pictured myself standing strong
And walking to the Jon
But still I laid there holding fast
To dreams I'd just dwelled on

I told my muscles to respond
But they didn't move a lick
The clock called out to poke my brain
Now counting off each tick

I finally bent right at the waist
And rose to see the mirror
And pulled myself to take a step
Just happy to be here

An Island?

No man is an island
Or is this not so?
For it seems that we are
When it's time to go
We face it alone
Even when someone's near
We face it with peace,
With grace or in fear
When darkness descends
Does it lighten a bit?
The second we die
Is it dark or well lit?
The ones we have loved
All now know for sure
The ones who have seen
What to us is a blur
We recall with grief
But somehow adjust
To the idea of loved ones
Returning to dust
No man is an island
Or is this not true?
For it seems that we are
On the day that we're through
To live life alone
Is a tragedy sure
But dying in solitude
How can one endure?
The undefined ending
The unknown respite
The conclusion of days

And the onset of night
To Adam He said 'tis
Not good all alone
Here is your helper now
Make her a home
And join yourself to her
And you join to him
Join fast to your woman
And you to your man
Live life together
Let no-one come in
Let nothing between you
Till death tries to win
And let it not take you
Not fear or despair
No man is an island
Look up I am there

Reality Check

Block the thought from your head
Spend no time on a dead-end street
Check yourself when the path you take
Leaves your mind controlled by your feet

Lock this thought in your head
Send no curse from your steps to your brain
Deck yourself when the road you choose
Puts the caboose in charge of the train

A Life Well Lived

There's no rust on a life well lived
No apologies, no decay, no regrets
No reason to fret at its passing
No talk of old lingering debts

A life well lived is forever
No trespass is ever relived
God delights in each moment that passes
In a faithful, and steady life lived

A life full of color and strength
In a world of grayness and hurt
A life that has made a creation
Out of tears, disappointment, and dirt

A life that's remembered by family
By friends and by strangers alike
A life less like a possession
And more like a sojourner's hike

A Number Between

I'm thinking of a number
Between one and three
A wondrous obsession of
You joining me
So guess if you will now
And turn "us" to "we"
By answering "yes," now
That you'll marry me!

Caught Between Two Seeds

We are caught between two seeds
One question to be raised
One question to be answered
Of faith or chance or deeds
Surely we are blessed with life
Surely we will last
Surely at the end of days
There's more than just our past

We are caught between two seeds
A dispermous lot are we
An Isaac and an Ishmael
In verse an epopee
Surely we are here for good
Surely cursed to cry
Surely at the end of days
We're surely cursed to die

We are caught between two seeds
Be fruitful or be food
Jejune-like creatures sitting here
In a jealous, senescent mood
Surely we are meant for more
Surely to make seed
Surely at the end of days
A flower not a weed

My Firefly

To capture your heart
A firefly
In humid night
Elusive
A boyish chase
Adventure
A dash through hidden woods
Dangerous
Through moss-filled fallen oaks
I reach for hidden ferns
Your light
Draws my hand
To hold you
In trembling boldness
Palms open to the sky
You delight me
So bright
So hard to catch
So now mine to hold

The Day Has Come

The day has come when we shall be joined
Together for all to see

But only you and I know the depth of our Love
There is no power other than God himself
Who can separate us and He has chosen
For us to live together as one

Greater love has no man, than he that would lay
His life down for his friend
You are my friend.

The joy of this day will soon turn into the
Tedious business of everyday living and raising
Our children

But the hardship will only test our love and
Show to all the world that it is pure

So on this day like many days before and
Many days to come, I give you all my love
And I am convinced that we will make it
Through the number of days, which God has
Given us, because there is nothing greater than love;
Ask Jesus; because of Him you shall be my wife
      And I shall be your husband.

Now Is Coming

He comes
He comes without wishing, He comes
He comes whether we watch or hide; He comes
He waits; or seems to wait for us to want Him to come
And for those that don't know
Come; come and light up the sky with certainty
Come; so all the waiting melts with the presence of Now
Come; and take first the sleeping in you, then us
Come; and let all who see know that you have come
And more for those who won't go

Free from Niggling

Be thou not a niggler
Blinded by details
Details vain and valueless
Like baskets filled with pails

Everyone is needed
But not for sucking thoughts
Some things must be left invisible
As affirmation's naughts

Be thou not a niggler
Niggling for a naughty treat
Niggling for amusement only
Niggling on a teat

Niggle not; but think it through
Questions pondered making blocks
An invisible firm cornerstone
Not sand or slippery rocks

But let the details serve you
And by them be not pained
Let the nigglers niggle
And be yourself unchained

Dirge of Dogs

Howl of dogs
Cuts the quiet night
Giving something, something
To offer focus
Though they soon will find me here

The silent notes
Of songs that long have stopped
Leaving quickly, quickly
From lips still moving
Though they soon will play a dirge

I hear my breath
A soulful rap without much melody
Fading surely, surely
From lips still moving, to offer focus
That the dirge will play for me

Simple Things

Simple things
Simply done
Simple melodies
Simply sung
Simple pleasures
Simply fun
Simple victories
Simply won
Simple love bells
Simply rung
Simple family
Simply run
Simple shadings
Simply sun
Simple sorrows
Simply none

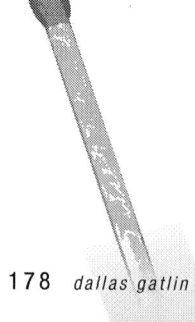

Speaking Frankly

Frankly speaking
I don't know you
Frankly speaking
I never will
Never mind that I'll always love you
And I hope with this honesty
You'll love me still

Chances are
You'll misunderstand this
Chances are
It'll make you weep
Keep in mind that you're my best friend
And I'm yours to forever keep

Truth be told
There's a wall between us
Truth be told
It's our human bane
But it's also that which makes us
Me and you with "us" to gain

So in the end
There's time to account for
In the end
Was it all well spent?
Frankly speaking there's none here owners
In the end, we all but rent

Yet speaking frankly
I do so know you
And though we're leasing
I always will
Keep in mind that I do love you
And I hope when we leave here
You'll love me still

The Wings that I Grew

The view is awesome
Awesome from here
Here where I'm safe but near
Near to the risk of losing it all
All for the chance to let go
Let go of the peace
That settles in quickly
Shed all the scales that protect
Molt from the armor
Emerging anew
New as a warrior with lift
Lift from new wings
That sprout from inside
Unfolded, once sheltered from blades
Blades that cut quickly, are quickly resheathed
As if no purpose was thought fore the lunge
The attack that was offered was only for fun
No thought for the object run through
No thought for the object run through
No mind that the thing is so fraught with chance
The chance that rejection will kill
The thing that I want
Is to ride up the lift
That comes with the wings that I grew
That comes with the wings that I grew

70 Sticks

70 sticks arranged all in fives
Not many sticks to number our lives
Each group of ten
One bunch at a time
Easily bundled in burnable size

CELESTE CLOTURE

Celeste, Celeste
We've talked it out
I've listened as you spoke
I've heard the words
That painted you in a corner
You had to see it coming
The hue is from your hand
It seems you wanted to be there
All along

Celeste, Celeste
You're calling me
I hear you and respond
I hear your words
But you're just still and sit there
Feel, the paint is dry
You stopped so long ago
It seems you want to stay there
Please decide

Celeste, Celeste
I'm coming for you
I've listened long enough
I've heard the words
That hold you in your prison
Repetition has you paralyzed
The verse is from your tongue yet
I know you want to be here, so
I come

Death in a Sesame Seed Bun

We lift them two handed with zeal
And raise them to lips open wide
We've declared this poison a meal
Denying that others have died!

More grease than a muscle car chassis
You might as well suck on a gun
It's gross, and nauseous, and nasty, it's
Death in a sesame seed bun!

In Some Ways

In some ways
I want to stay right where I am
In some ways
I want to take her by the hand and
Taking her alone
Leave all we've accumulated
Behind
In some ways
It would be fresh, like new snow
In some ways
It would re-initialize a cluttered
Hard drive and
Erase the viruses that slow us
Down
In some ways
I want to stay right here where I am
In some ways
I want to hold her and
Just turn to her in bed
And accumulate one more
Moment

Camouflaged Cookies

Camouflaged cookies all freshly made
Baked for to share, before the thoughts fade
Timely investment
But timeliness not
Delivery not made because you forgot

Maybe tomorrow, is quite good enough
To share what you think, with someone beloved
Sadly mistaken
Mistaken in thought
Goodly intentions but kindness for naught

Never detected, and therefore not seen
Your kindly intentions, not one of them mean
But meanness perceived
In kindness not shared
Camouflaged cookies, who knew that you cared?

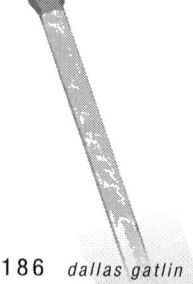

INSIDE GOD

Have you ever wondered?
What's inside God?
Infinitely big, infinitely small?
Endlessly short, endlessly tall?
Everything made, all inside all?

Have you ever pondered?
Where God now resides?
Beyond the known universe, inside your heart?
At the end of all things, before the start?
Outside all that matters, yet inside each part?

Have you ever considered?
That we are inside?
Created to be there, created to see?
Created just like Him, and like him to be?
But living outside Him, like God should be me?

Perhaps we have blundered?
About what's in God?
Inside His heart, inside His mind?
Infinitely patient, lovingly kind?
Easy to go to, easy to find?

Leave Gold Behind

Leave some gold behind
Behind you as you leave
Plan it out ahead of time
To honor your bereaved

Honor them with providence
Feed not the hungry moths
Leave gold and not the rusting stuff
That wastes like fading cloths

Deeds of love and
Deeds of faith
Deeds of sacrifice
Words of peace and
Words of grace
Words of fragrant spice

Leave some gold behind
To your wife and kids and friends
Work it out ahead of time
Beginnings made of ends

Honor all with a picture
Of Christ seen in a mirror
A life, a death, a mixture
To hold from year to year

NADI

I Nadi to a place in five
A place?
Well maybe not
A time or locus
Lame words to say
Not square, nor sphere, nor dot
I move a breath, and overcome
The chains that hold me here
And leave this bane of three or four
To Nadi something near
It is while there or then or what
That clearness comes to me
Or I to it, or both to one
At least it's now I see
I Nadi to a vision live
In space?
Well probably not
A sense, a knowing
Bringing gifts
Back to my life, a dot

People Are

People are precious
They hug when they arrive
And when they go
So many hurts and wants
And wishes and fears of hurts
And wishes
I see them, some know
I'm watching, some feel it
So precious, so many, so busy
Each has plans, to do good
Or evil, or nothing
But they move, each one
From here to there
Slowly, suddenly
People are precious and lovely
Lowly and exalted
And they are lovely all
Looking for people
To hold them, to listen
To them
And without words to affirm
That they are
Precious

Promises Unkempt

Don't stand there
Looking in the mirror
Unless you're willing to look askance at
The "you" you've decided now to feature
The you who vowed, but now recants
What visitor has mused you?
Who rang there at the door?
Why do you act as if the house is empty?
And primp there like a whore?
You look, you turn
You purse your lips
Whom do you seek to temp?
Standing there, intentions bare
And promises unkempt

Purple Target

It was always my aim to hit the mark
To take my time, allow for the wind
I dreamed of sighting it in
To stare deep into its center
Hold my breath, and let go my grip
I knew once I had committed
I would not, could not
Call back the shot
So I was careful, deliberate
And took my time
I could see it, day and night
The seeing warmed me
I never thought of it moving
It was always there until it moved
Without warning, moved
In my mind I had placed a ring
Around it, not to claim it or
Hold it, but to tell it in a way
I had focused on it
For a moment and a moment only
I lost sight of it
Then, after a time, there it was, purple
There she was
I aimed, and let the arrow fly

She Provides

She partners with God
She provides
For our children she rises
And loves them by hand
She makes our house, "home"
She provides
With quiet persistence
She provides
For her husband she rises
And loves him by hand
She's the rhythm of this poem
She provides
She is flowers and sun
She provides
Each new day she rises
And loves life by hand
I'm never alone
She provides

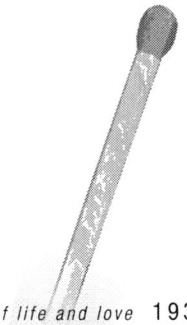

The Cosmos Question

The cosmos is big
Or something like that
Billions and billions of stars
Trillions of galaxies
Across empty space
Comets and quasars and Mars

The cosmos is tiny
Or something like that
Electrons and protons and quarks
People who wonder
And others who don't
Geniuses, preachers, and dorks

The cosmos is mysterious
Or something like that
Designed or an accident of fate
A time and a place
Provided by grace?
We question, we listen, we wait

What Do I Know?

What do I know, about anything?
I look at my hands; they're mine
My feet seem less mine
But there they are, attached
I know my mother, but only in a fog
And not really her
But my "her"
A bit like I know my feet
So what *do* I know?
My mind? I guess
I do wonder what it looks like
From the outside in
Do I know God?
I know what my mind knows
Whether inside out or outside in
I cannot tell
So what do I know? For sure
I know I am writing, to someone
And when they read this
I hope they say,
"I know him and me"
So who do I know?

Who Created Whom?

Who created whom?
Was it chance or a big boom?
A zip and then a zoom?
Or maybe not

Who made the twinkling stars?
And the fireflies we put in jars?
Who created them?
Maybe God

Who created what?
The apple or the nut?
God prepared all these
Or maybe not

Who made the sun we chase?
And the planets out in space?
Maybe God or maybe chance
But thanks a lot

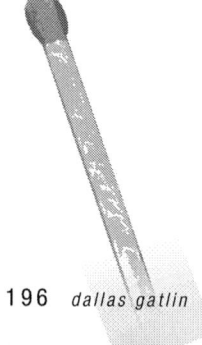

Now I created me I think
And you created you
In the atom is our glue
Or maybe not

Who created whom?
Is the question we should ask
Instead of make believing we all know
I know you made not me
And I know I didn't you
So let's just get that straight
Before we go!

Who created what or
What created whom?
The most important thing to comprehend
So ask it often daily
Let his spirit overtake thee
We'll all know all the answers
In the end

The Art of the Finish

So much indeed I do not know
Waiting for the gun to go off
Standing here wondering
If I'll have it today
As I expel all my doubts with a cough

The finals have come, and I'm here in the box
Staring at the grass out ahead
Bouncing a little
And ejecting some spittle
Will my legs become pistons or lead?

All is now silent, except in my head
As I talk to myself and my "friend"
There's another of me
Whom no-one can see
And he'll talk to me right to the end

The shot pierces silence, as we lurch from the line
And stretch to get first to the turn
I hear myself breathe
Four hundred lungs heave
Already there's cause for concern

My legs feel heavy and no friend to me
I'll have to earn this one I know
It's all runners' curse
You train and rehearse
To run down each friend and each foe

But my friend says, "You know you can't do it,
You're tired, you're tight, and you're slow,
The temperatures 90,
Treat yourself kindly,
Give up now and let the thing go"

My friend is persuasive, convincing
My mind sees me stopping right here
I've rehearsed what I'll say
And they'll all say, "Hey,
Better luck man, you'll do it next year"

Then my friend says, "Your dad, what's he thinking,
Disappointed you're not peaking today?
Man I think you should stop,
Declare this a flop,
And start thinking about what you will say"

My friend's voice is getting much louder
But no way will I listen and quit
Though the challenge has changed
My goal rearranged
I'll send my friend back to his pit

So I breathe though my lungs also fight me
Yet with focus my friend's tauntings diminish
And I've beat him today
Kept his cruel voice at bay
There's life in the art of the finish

Tate Publishing & *Enterprises*

Tate Publishing is commited to excellence in the publishing industry. Our staff of highly trained professionals, including editors, graphic designers, and marketing personnel, work together to produce the very finest books available. The company reflects the philosophy established by the founders, based on Psalms 68:11,

"THE LORD GAVE THE WORD AND GREAT WAS THE COMPANY OF THOSE WHO PUBLISHED IT."

If you would like further information, please call
1.888.361.9473
or visit our website
www.tatepublishing.com

TATE PUBLISHING & *Enterprises*, LLC
127 E. Trade Center Terrace
Mustang, Oklahoma 73064 USA